892

D1298500

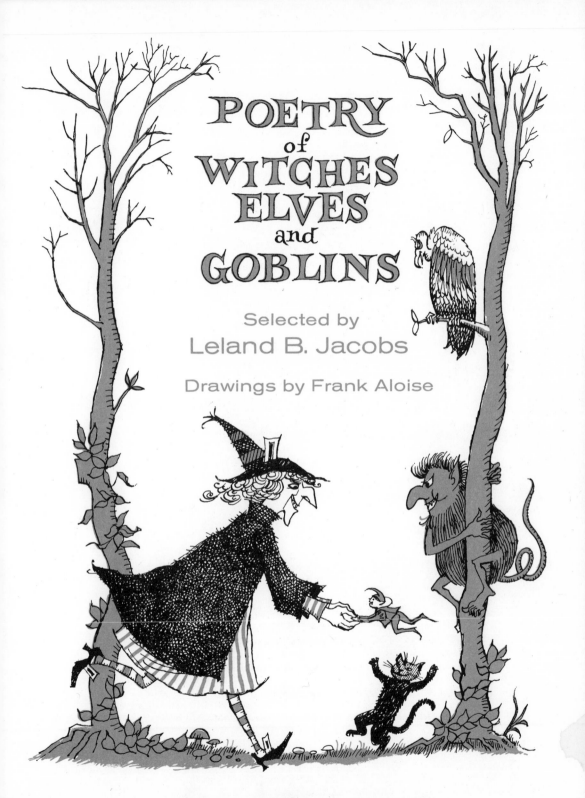

POETRY of WITCHES ELVES and GOBLINS

Selected by
Leland B. Jacobs

Drawings by Frank Aloise

GARRARD PUBLISHING COMPANY
CHAMPAIGN, ILLINOIS

j394.2
P 752

The editor and publisher acknowledge with thanks permission received to reprint the poems in this collection.

Acknowledgments and formal notices of copyright for all material under copyright appear on pages 61 and 62 which are hereby made an extension of the copyright page.

Copyright © 1970 by Leland B. Jacobs

All rights reserved. Manufactured in the U.S.A.

Standard Book Number: 8116-4105-8

Library of Congress Catalog Card Number: 70-99767

CONTENTS

Introductory Poems 5

About Witches 9

About Elves 15

About Brownies 23

About Goblins 28

About Giants 34

About Fairies 36

About Leprechauns 50

About Other Wee Folk . . 53

Closing Poems 58

Fay Folks

A brownie child,
　　A dwarf, a sprite
Can dance in print
　　On pages white.

A goblin, giant,
　　Troll, or gnome
Can claim a book
　　To be his home.

A fairy queen,
　　A woodland elf
Can live in books
　　Upon the shelf.

Unknown

From . . . .
Pipes and Drums

A little Pixie Piper went
    A-piping through the glens;
Some folks who heard him thought
    his notes
A robin's or a wren's.

"How late to hear a robin sing,
    It must be nearly ten!"
(The Pixie Piper chuckled and
    Went piping down the glen.)

"It wasn't quite a robin's note,
    I fancy 'twas a wren."
(The Pixie Piper chuckled and
 Went piping down the glen.)

If we'd been there we might have made
    The same mistakes ourselves:
The only folks who knew the truth
    Were Goblins, Gnomes, and Elves.

Lilian Holmes

What They Said

I am the old witch
Who lives by· the wall,
And I have come to snatch you—
To snatch you, one and all.

I am the goblin
Who lives by the stall,
And I have come to fetch you—
To fetch you, one and all.

I am the ghostie
Who lives in the hall,
And I have come to catch you—
To catch you, one and all.

Old Rhyme

About Witches

Witch Ways

In pointed hat
And flowing cloak,
The witches cackle,
Scream, and croak.

Way past the moon,
In the midnight sky,
The witches fly.
They fly! They fly!

In flowing cloak
And pointed hat,
They stir their brew
Of toad and gnat.

Then—having supped—
In the midnight sky,
The witches fly.
They fly! They fly!

Anonymous

POISON IVY!

A wicked witch
Is Mizzable Scratch,
And it's **TROUBLE** she grows
In her garden patch.
And her garden patch
Lies all around,
For she grows Poison Ivy!

By ditch and fence
She leaves her trail,
As she sows her seed
Over hill and dale,
And her crop of mischief
Can never fail,
For she grows Poison Ivy!

So listen, my children,
Take heed, be good,
And if ever you roam
Through a tangled wood,
Or follow a road,
Some lovely day,
Over the hills and far away,
Please keep out
Of the garden patch
Sown and grown by Mizzable Scratch,
Or it's TROUBLE you will surely catch,
For she grows Poison Ivy!

Katherine Gallagher

Witch, Witch

'Witch, witch, where do you fly?' . . .
'Under the clouds and over the sky.'

'Witch, witch, what do you eat?' . . .
'Little black apples from Hurricane Street.'

'Witch, witch, what do you drink?' . . .
'Vinegar, blacking, and good red ink.'

'Witch, witch, where do you sleep?' . . .
'Up in the clouds where pillows are cheap.'

Rose Fyleman

Beware

Beware the witch's magic glance!
    One look into her eye
Will turn you to a broomstick,
    To ride the midnight sky.

Beware the witch's magic brew,
    For but a taste of that
Will turn you quite immediately
    Into a big, black cat.

Beware the witch's magic power,
    Beware the witch's spell,
Lest when you'll be yourself again,
    Who can ever tell?

Lee Blair

Bittersweet

Bittersweet,
Bittersweet,
Bittersweet blue.
A young witch
Danced deep in
Last night's silver dew.
And where her feet
Tripped on
The green grassy floor,
You came up,
With nightshades
And toadstools galore!

Bittersweet,
Bittersweet,
Bittersweet blue,
Printed by
Witch's feet
Deep in the dew.

Ivy O. Eastwick

The Little Elf

I met a little Elfman, once,
    Down where the lilies blow.
I asked him why he was so small,
    And why he didn't grow.

He slightly frowned, and with his eye
    He looked me through and through.
"I'm quite as big for me," said he,
    "As you are big for you."

John Kendrick Bangs

The Seven Ages Of Elf-Hood

When an Elf is as old as a year and a minute
He can wear a cap with a feather in it.

By the time that he is two times two
He has a buckle for either shoe.

At twenty he is fine as a fiddle,
With a little brown belt to go round his middle.

When he's lived for fifty years or so
His coat may have buttons all in a row.

If past three score and ten he's grown
Two pockets he has for his very own.

At eighty-two or three years old
They bulge and jingle with bits of gold.

But when he's a hundred and a day
He gets a little pipe to play!

Rachel Field

Elves' Song

When the night winds sigh,
    And the sun is hid,
And the fireflies fly,
    And the Katydid
Begins to fiddle a merry tune,
    We sit in a ring,
And we laugh and sing,
    We chant and we croon
In the light of the moon,
    In the silvery slivers
Of the light of the moon.

B. J. Lee

The Elfin Plane

The dragonfly who hurries by
    With hum that never varies
Is like an airplane in the sky
    To elfin folk and fairies.
His motor stops, his motor starts
    Without a bit of stalling.
His engine is his heart of hearts
    And needs no overhauling.

Rowena Bennett

The Elf
And The Dormouse

Under a toadstool
    Crept a wee Elf,
Out of the rain
    To shelter himself.

Under the toadstool,
    Sound asleep,
Sat a big Dormouse
    All in a heap.

Trembled the wee Elf,
   Frightened, and yet
Fearing to fly away
   Lest he get wet..

To the next shelter—
   Maybe a mile!
Sudden the wee Elf
   Smiled a wee smile.

Tugged till the toadstool
   Toppled in two,
Holding it over him,
   Gaily he flew.

Soon he was safe home,
   Dry as could be.
Soon woke the Dormouse—
   "Good gracious me!

"Where is my toadstool?"
   Loud he lamented.
And that's how umbrellas
   First were invented.

Oliver Herford

The Harvest Elves

The harvesters–they say themselves–
Are haunted by the harvest elves.

These elves–they say–as small as dolls
Have poppies for their parasols.

And when you hear the swish of stalks
It's elves a-sweeping their green walks.

And so when next a field you cross
And see the wheat-ears roll and toss,

Go quietly, and if you peep
Maybe you'll find an elf asleep

Inside a little hammock-bed,
Just as the harvesters have said.

Wilfrid Thorley

Where Brownies Are

Brownies on the hillside,
Brownies in the glen,
Are wee little, free little
Gleeful men,
Running up the hillside,
Skipping in the dell.
I have met the brownie folk—
I know them well.

Anonymous

The Brownies' Year

The brownies are a happy folk—
    A happy folk are they.
In summer, down among the ferns,
    At hide and seek they play.

In autumn, when the thistle down
    Is much like silvery hair,
Across the open fields they ride
    All in the golden air.

In winter, when the cold is come,
　　They sit at home and sup
On maple sap and icicle juice
　　From out an acorn cup.

In spring, the brownies scurry out,
　　To greet each sunny day.
The brownies are a happy folk—
　　A happy folk are they.

Anonymous

25

Jamboree

The wind told the willow,
    And the willow told me,
"Tonight's the night the brownie folk
    Will hold a jamboree.
They'll dance to a cricket band,
    They'll sing brownie tunes,
And some of them will take a ride
    In thistledown balloons.
They'll bob for thorn apples,
    They'll sip fresh dew."
And everything the willow said
    Came absolutely true.

Lee Blair

What I Think

As I was sitting
by a bush,
a small, hushed sound I heard.
I think it was
a brownie
who had said a brownie word.

As I was standing
in the woods,
nuts showered from a tree.
I think it was
a brownie prank
to pelt some nuts at me.

As moonlight streamed
across the lawn,
a darting shadow sped.
I'm sure it was
a brownie child
scampering off to bed.

Lee Blair

A Goblinade

A green hobgoblin,
    Small but quick,
Went out walking
    With a black thorn stick

He was full of mischief,
    Full of glee.
He frightened all
    That he could see.

He saw a little maiden
    In a wood.
He looked as fierce as
    A goblin should.

He crept by the hedge row,
    He said, "Boo!"
"Boo!" laughed the little girl,
    "How are you?"

"What!" said the goblin,
    "Aren't you afraid?"
"I think you're funny,"
    Said the maid.

"Ha!" said the goblin,
    Sitting down flat.
"You think I'm funny?
    I don't like that."

Florence Page Jaques

The Treat

The buttercup in the meadow
    Catches the sun's bright gold,
And catches the morning dew drops,
    As many as it can hold.

The buttercup mixes sunshine
    With dew in its goblet. Then
Offers its rare sweet beverage
    To thirsty goblin men.

When I have been out walking
    In August's mid-day heat,
Oh, would I were a goblin
    To taste so rare a treat!

Lee Blair

Three Ghostesses

Three little ghostesses,
Sitting on postesses,
Eating buttered toastesses,
Greasing their fistesses,
Up to their wristesses,
Oh, what beastesses
To make such feastesses!

Old Rhyme

Autumn
Ghost Sounds

When the moon
rides high,
up overhead—
and I am snug
and warm,
in bed—
in the autumn dark
the ghosts move 'round,
making their
mournful,
moaning sound.

I listen to know
when the ghosts
go by.
I hear a wail,
and I hear
a sigh.
But I can't quite tell
which I hear
the most—
the wind,
or the wail
of some passing ghost.

Anonymous

Ghost Weather

This foggy night
The ghosts will be out.
In billowy white
This foggy night
The ghosts will delight
In gliding about.
You'd better beware.
You'd better take care.
In billowy white
The ghosts will be out,
To wander about,
And fill you with fright,
This foggy night,
This foggy night.

Lee Blair

Giant

One foot in the river,
    One foot in the lake—
What wonderful strides
    A giant can take!

The water goes "Squish"
    When he wiggles his toes.
Oh, giants have fun,
    As anyone knows.

His red rubber boots
    Reach up to his knee.
Why, puddles are nothing
    To giants like me!

Elizabeth Sawyer

Thunder

Do you know
What thunder is?
Beyond those clouds
So gray,
A giant's children
Slammed a door,
And skipped around
The sky to play
In quite a
Helter-skelter way.
So when you hear
The thunder, there
Are giant's children
In the air.

B. J. Lee

The Child And The Fairies

The woods are full of fairies!
   The trees are all alive:
The river overflows with them,
   See how they dip and dive!
What funny little fellows!
   What dainty little dears!
They dance and leap, and prance and peep,
   And utter fairy cheers!

Anonymous

36

If You See A Fairy Ring

If you see a fairy ring
    In a field of grass,
Very lightly step around,
    Tiptoe as you pass;
Last night fairies frolicked there,
And they're sleeping somewhere near.

If you see a tiny fay
    Lying fast asleep,
Shut your eyes and run away,
    Do not stay to peep;
And be sure you never tell,
Or you'll break a fairy spell.

Anonymous

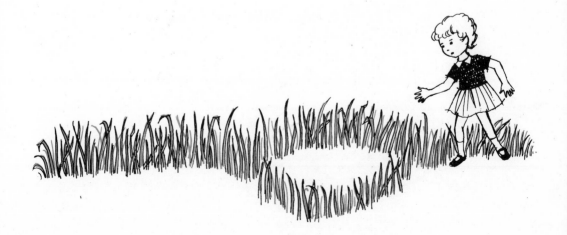

From .... Queen Mab

A little fairy comes at night;
    Her eyes are blue, her hair is brown,
With silver spots upon her wings,
    And from the moon she flutters down.

She has a little silver wand,
    And when a good child goes to bed
She waves her hand from right to left
    And makes a circle round its head.

And then it dreams of pleasant things:
    Of fountains filled with fairy fish,
And trees that bear delicious fruit,
    And bend their branches at a wish;

And talking birds with gifted tongues
    For singing songs and telling tales;
And funny dwarfs to show the way
    Through fairy hills and fairy dales.

Thomas Hood

City Fairies

Fairies live in forests
And have tremendous larks,
But there are city fairies, too,
Who much prefer the parks.

Merry-go-rounds are their rings—
Why dance when they can ride?
They think the forest fairies
Are slow and countrified.

Mildred Bowers Armstrong

From . . . .
I See the Fairies

Oh, I can see the fairies small
    'Most everywhere I look,
For one can find some beauty hid
    In every little nook.

For this is what the fairies are:
    The souls of lovely things,
And anywhere that beauty is
    A fairy laughs and sings.

Edrie MacFarland

The Light-Hearted Fairy

Oh, who is so merry, so merry, heigh ho!
As the light-hearted fairy? Heigh-ho,
    Heigh ho!
  He dances and sings
  To the sound of his wings
With a hey and a high and a ho!

Oh, who is so merry, so merry, heigh ho!
As the light-footed fairy? Heigh ho,
    Heigh ho!
  The night is his noon
  And his sun is the moon,
With a hey and a high and a ho!

Unknown

Fairy Washing

The fairies hung their washing out,
    Their linens and their laces,
And some of them were raggedy
    And very torn in places.

But busy old Dame Spider
    Brought out her silver thread
And darned each dainty tablecloth
    And mended every spread.

The fairies were so happy
    They said, "You dear old spinner!
We'll set the toadstool table now
    And you must stay for dinner."

Rowena Bennett

Fairy Shoes

The little shoes of fairies are
   So light and soft and small
That though a million pass you by
   You would not hear at all.

Annette Wynne

Fairies

  The fairies, it is said
Drop maple leaves into the stream
   To dye their waters red.

Kikaku

Finding Fairies

When the winds of March are wakening
    The crocuses and crickets,
Did you ever find a fairy near
    Some budding little thickets,
A-straightening her golden wings and
    Combing out her hair?
        She's there!

And when she sees you creeping up
    To get a closer peek,
She tumbles through the daffodils,
    A-playing hide-and-seek,
And creeps into the tulips till
    You can't find where she's hid?
        Mine did!

Have you ever, ever come across
    A little toadstool elf
A-reading by a firefly lamp
    And laughing to himself,
Or a saucy fairy queen upon
    Her favorite dragonfly?
        So've I!

It's fun to see a fairy flutter
    Off a catskin boat,
And wrap her fairy baby in
    A pussywillow coat;
Oh, don't you love the fairies
    And their fairy babies too?
        I do!

Marjorie Barrows

Fairy Voyage

If I were just a fairy small,
    I'd take a leaf and sail away,
I'd sit astride the stem and guide
    It straight to Fairyland—and stay.

Unknown

Merrily Float

A lake and a fairy boat
To sail in the moonlight clear—
And merrily we would float
From the dragons that watch us here!

Thomas Hood

Magic Vine

A fairy seed I planted,
So dry and white and old;
There sprang a vine enchanted
With magic flowers of gold.

I watched it, I tended it,
And truly, by and by,
It bore a Jack-O-Lantern,
And a great Thanksgiving pie.

Unknown

The Best Game
the Fairies Play

The best game the fairies play,
    The best game of all,
Is sliding down steeples—
    (You know they're very tall).
You fly to the weathercock,
    And when you hear it crow
You fold your wings and clutch your things
    And then let go!

They have a million other games—
    Cloud-catching's one,
And mud-mixing after rain
    Is heaps and heaps of fun;
But when you go and stay with them
    Never mind the rest,
Take my advice—they're very nice,
    But steeple-sliding's best!

Rose Fyleman

Could It Have Been a Shadow?

What ran under the rosebush?
    What ran under the stone?
Could it have been a shadow,
    Running away alone?
Maybe a fairy's shadow,
    Slipping away at dawn
To guard a gleaming pot of gold
    For a busy leprechaun.

Monica Shannon

Faith, I Wish I Were
a Leprechaun

Faith, I wish I were a leprechaun
Beneath a hawthorn tree,
A-cobblin' of wee, magic boots,
A-eatin' luscious, lovely fruits;
Oh, fiddle-dum, oh, fiddle-dee,
I wish I were a leprechaun
Beneath a hawthorn tree!

Faith, I wish I were a leprechaun
Beneath a hawthorn tree,
A-throwin' snuff into the eyes
Of young and old and dull and wise;
Oh, fiddle-dum, oh, fiddle-dee,
I wish I were a leprechaun
Beneath a hawthorn tree!

Faith, I wish I were a leprechaun
Beneath a hawthorn tree,
With no more irksome thing to do
Than sew a small, bewitchin' shoe;
Oh, fiddle-dum, oh, fiddle-dee,
I wish I were a leprechaun
Beneath a hawthorn tree!

Margaret Ritter

The Leprechaun

Up he is, at the break of dawn,
A busy, gleeful leprechaun,
Making shoes so fine and small—
Though human folks can't hear at all
His hammer tapping, or the song
He sings to help his work along.

Up he is, in the mossy glen,
Designing shoes for elfin men.
With silver nails and platinum thread
He pounds and sews, while in his head
He recollects the wee folk, whose
So silent feet now wear his shoes.

Lee Blair

Troll Trick

With many a scowl
And many a frown,
A troll pushed
Stones and boulders down.

The crashing sound
Made town folks wonder:
Is it a troll
Or is it thunder?

But hill folks knew.
When boulders roll,
It's always the trick
Of a terrible troll.

B. J. Lee

The Gnome

I saw a Gnome
As plain as plain
Sitting on top
Of a weathervane.

He was dressed like a crow
In silky black feathers,
And there he sat watching
All kinds of weathers.

He talked like a crow too,
Caw caw caw,
When he told me exactly
What he saw,

Snow to the north of him
Sun to the south,
And he spoke with a beaky
Kind of a mouth.

But he wasn't a crow,
That was plain as plain
'Cause crows never sit
On a weathervane.

What I saw was simply
A usual gnome
Looking things over
On his way home.

Harry Behn

54

Dwarf's Lullabye

Sleep, my child,
For the night is mild,
And the moon is a fairy white.
Lay down your head
On your mossy bed.
Goodnight! Goodnight! Goodnight!

Sleep, my dear,
For the night is clear,
And the fireflies flash their light.
Stretch out upon
Your thistledown.
Goodnight! Goodnight! Goodnight!

Sleep, my pet,
For the sun is set,
And that shadow's just a sprite.
You've drunk your dew.
Sleep the whole night through.
Goodnight! Goodnight! Goodnight!

B. J. Lee

Frost Sprite

The frost sprite always
    Thinks it's fun
To play his pranks
    On everyone.

He pinches ears,
    And cheeks, and toes,
But where he's standing
    No-one knows.

He paints upon
    The window pane:
A flower, a bridge,
    A vine, a chain.

He nips the leaves
    Upon the trees,
This busy fellow
    No-one sees.

Unknown

From . . . .
The Fairies

Up the airy mountain,
    Down the rushy glen,
We daren't go a-hunting
    For fear of little men;
Wee folk, good folk,
    Trooping all together;
Green jacket, red cap,
    And white owl's feather!

Down along the rocky shore
    Some make their home;
They live on crispy pancakes
    Of yellow tide-foam;
Some in the reeds
    Of the black mountain-lake,
With frogs for their watch-dogs,
    All night awake.

By the craggy hillside,
  Through the mosses bare,
They have planted thorn-trees
  For pleasure here and there.
Is any man so daring
  As dig them up in spite,
He shall find their sharpest thorns
  In his bed at night.

Up the airy mountain,
  Down the rushy glen,
We daren't go a-hunting
  For fear of little men;
Wee folk, good folk,
  Trooping all together;
Green jacket, red cap,
  And white owl's feather!

William Allingham

59

One Saturday Night

One Saturday night
I lost my way,
And into the forest
I chanced to stray,
And there in the woods
Were folks so wee
Their faces and features
I never did see.
They paid no heed,
For I stood quite still.
They went on dancing
With such a will,
With such abandon,
With such delight,
I skipped clear home
That Saturday night.

Anonymous

Acknowledgments

Detroit Free Press for permission to reprint from "I See Fairies" by Edrie Mac-Farland from *The Ship of Silver*, Copyright 1925.

Doubleday & Company Inc. for permission to reprint "Could It Have Been a Shadow" from *Goose Grass Rhymes* by Monica Shannon. Copyright 1930 by Doubleday & Company Inc. Also for "The Best Games the Fairies Play" from *Fairies and Chimneys* by Rose Fyleman. Copyright 1918, 1920 by Doubleday & Company Inc. Also for "Witch, Witch" from *Fifty-one New Nursery Rhymes* by Rose Fyleman, Copyright 1932 by Doubleday & Company Inc.

Follett Publishing Company for permission to reprint "The Elfin Plane" from *The Day is Dancing* by Rowena Bennett. Text copyright © 1948, 1968 by Rowena Bennett.

Harcourt, Brace & World, Inc. for permission to reprint "The Gnome" from *Windy Morning* by Harry Behn, copyright 1953.

George G. Harrap & Company Limited for permission to reprint "The Harvest Elves" by Wilfrid Thorley from *The Happy Colt* published by George G. Harrap & Company Limited.

The Instructor for permission to reprint "Giant" by Elizabeth Sawyer, published in *Poems Children Enjoy* by The Instructor Publications, Inc., 1962.

Jack and Jill Magazine © 1948 The Curtis Publishing Company for special permission to reprint "Poison Ivy" by Katherine Gallagher.

Florence Page Jaques for her poem "A Goblinade" from *Child Life Magazine*, Copyright 1927, 1955 by Rand McNally & Company.

J. B. Lippincott Company for permission to reprint "Fairy Shoes" by Annette Wynne from the book *For Days and Days* by Annette Wynne. Copyright 1919, 1947 by Annette Wynne.

David McKay Company Inc. for permission to reprint "Bittersweet" from *Traveler's Joy* by Ivy O. Eastwick. Copyright © 1960, by Ivy O. Eastwick.

The Macmillan Company for permission to reprint "The Seven Ages of Elf-Hood" from *Poems* by Rachel Field. Copyright by The Macmillan Company, renewed 1954 by Arthur S. Pederson. Also for "Faith, I Wish I Were a Leprechaun" from *Collected Poems* by Margaret T. Ritter. Copyright 1925 by The Macmillan Company, renewed 1953 by Margaret T. Ritter.

Rand McNally & Company for permission to reprint "Finding Fairies" from *Read-Aloud Poems Every Young Child Should Know* compiled by Marjorie Barrows. Copyright 1957 by Rand McNally & Company. Also for "City Fairies" by Mildred Bowers Armstrong from *Child Life Magazine*, copyright 1931, 1959 by Rand McNally & Company.

Meredith Press and Appleton-Century-Crofts for permission to reprint "The Elf and the Dormouse" by Oliver Herford from *A St. Nicholas Anthology*. Copyright © 1969 by Meredith Corporation. Also for "The Little Elf" by John Kendrick Bangs from *A St. Nicholas Anthology*. Copyright © 1969 by Meredith Corporation.

Oxford University Press for permission to reprint from "Pipes and Drums" by Lilian Holmes from *Mrs. Strang's Annual for Children*. Also for "Fairies" by Kikaku from *A Year of Japanese Epigrams* by William N. Porter, known in the original as "The Fairies and the Maple Leaves," published by the Oxford University Press.

Plays, Inc. Publishers, for permission to reprint "Fairy Washing" from *Creative Plays and Programs for Holidays* by Rowena Bennett. Copyright © 1966 by Rowena Bennett, Plays, Inc., Publishers, Boston, Mass. 02116

61

Index of Authors

Allingham, William
from The Fairies 58

Armstrong, Mildred Bowers
City Fairies 39

Bangs, John Kendrick
The Little Elf 15

Barrows, Marjorie
Finding Fairies 44

Behn, Harry
The Gnome 54

Bennett, Rowena
The Elfin Plane 19
Fairy Washing 42

Blair, Lee
Beware 13
Jamboree 26
What I Think 27
The Treat 30
Ghost Weather 33
The Leprechaun 52

Eastwick, Ivy O.
Bittersweet 14

Field, Rachel
The Seven Ages of
Elf-Hood 16

Fyleman, Rose
Witch, Witch 12
The Best Game the
Fairies Play 48

Gallagher, Katherine
Poison Ivy! 10

Herford, Oliver
The Elf and the
Dormouse 20

Holmes, Lilian
from Pipes and Drums 6

Hood, Thomas
from Queen Mab 38
Merrily Float 46

Jaques, Florence Page
A Goblinade 28

Kikaku
Fairies 43

Lee, B. J.
Elves' Song 18
Thunder 35
Troll Trick 53
Dwarf's Lullabye 56

MacFarland, Edrie
from I See the Fairies 40

Ritter, Margaret
Faith, I Wish I Were
a Leprechaun 50

Sawyer, Elizabeth
Giant 34

Shannon, Monica
Could It Have Been
a Shadow? 49

Thorley, Wilfrid
  The Harvest Elves 22

Wynne, Annette
  Fairy Shoes 43

Unknown
  Fay Folks 5
  What They Said 8
  Witch Ways 9
  Where Brownies Are 23
  The Brownies' Year 24

Three Ghostesses 31
Autumn Ghost Sounds 32
The Child and
  the Fairies 36
If You See a Fairy Ring 37
The Light-Hearted Fairy 41
Fairy Voyage 46
Magic Vine 47
Frost Sprite 57
One Saturday Night 60